T0080930

# The Pocket Stoic

# The Pocket Stoic
John Sellars

THE UNIVERSITY OF CHICAGO PRESS

The University of Chicago Press, Chicago 60637
© 2019 by John Sellars
The moral right of the author has been asserted.
All rights reserved. No part of this book may be used or
reproduced in any manner whatsoever without written
permission, except in the case of brief quotations in critical
articles and reviews. For more information, contact the
University of Chicago Press, 1427 E. 60th St., Chicago, IL 60637.
Published 2020
Printed in the United States of America

29 28 27 26 25 24 23      3 4 5

ISBN-13: 978-0-226-68296-9 (cloth)
ISBN-13: 978-0-226-68301-0 (e-book)
DOI: https://doi.org/10.7208/chicago/9780226683010.001.0001

First published by Allen Lane, an imprint of Penguin
Random House UK, 2019.

Library of Congress Cataloging-in-Publication Data

Names: Sellars, John, 1971– author.
Title: The pocket stoic / John Sellars.
Description: Chicago : The University of Chicago Press, 2020. |
    Includes bibliographical references.
Identifiers: LCCN 2019018460 | ISBN 9780226682969 (cloth : alk. paper)
    | ISBN 9780226683010 (e-book)
Subjects: LCSH: Stoics. | Seneca, Lucius Annaeus, approximately 4
    B.C.–65 A.D. | Epictetus. | Marcus Aurelius, Emperor of Rome,
    121–180. | Philosophy, Ancient.
Classification: LCC B528 .S2978 2019 | DDC 188 – dc23
LC record available at https://lccn.loc.gov/2019018460

♾ This paper meets the requirements of ANSI/NISO Z39.48-1992
(Permanence of Paper).

# Contents

# Prologue

**WHAT IF SOMEONE** told you that much of
the suffering in your life was simply due
to the way you think about things? I don't
mean physical suffering like pain or hunger,
but all the other things that can negatively
colour one's life: anxiety, frustration, fear,
disappointment, anger, general discontent.
What if someone claimed that they could
show you how to avoid all of this? And what
if they said that these things were in fact the
product of looking at the world in a mistaken
way? What if it turned out that the ability

to avoid all of these things was completely within your control?

These are all claims that we find in the works of the three great Roman Stoics – Seneca, Epictetus and Marcus Aurelius – who lived in the first and second centuries AD. Seneca is remembered for his role as tutor to the Emperor Nero, Epictetus was a slave who gained his freedom and went on to set up a philosophical school, while Marcus Aurelius was Emperor of Rome. Their lives could not have been more different, and yet they all embraced Stoicism as a guide to how to live well.

By the time our three Roman Stoics were writing, Stoicism was already hundreds of years old. It all began in Athens. The founder of the school was called Zeno, originally from Cyprus. He was the son of a merchant who, on one account, visited Athens shortly before 300 BC to conduct business for his father. While there, he came into contact with philosophers in the city, and soon began studying with masters from a number of competing schools. Rather than committing himself to any one of these philosophies, he decided to become a teacher in his own right and started to lecture at the Painted Stoa – a covered colonnade – in the centre of Athens. He quickly gathered a number of followers, who soon came to be known as Stoics – the people who gathered at the Painted Stoa. The Stoic school developed under Zeno's successors Cleanthes and Chrysippus, both of whom came to Athens from Asia Minor. Subsequent Stoics came from ever further east, such as Diogenes of Babylon. None of the works of these early Stoics survived past the end of antiquity, never making the transition from ancient papyrus scrolls to medieval parchment manuscripts, and what we know of their thought is based on quotations and summaries by later authors.

For our three Roman Stoics, by contrast, we have substantial literary remains. In the case of Seneca, we have essays on a range of philosophical topics, a set of letters to his friend Lucilius, and a number of tragedies. For Epictetus we have a series of discourses written by his pupil Arrian that purport to record lectures from his school, along with a short handbook that digests some key themes from those discourses. With Marcus Aurelius we have something quite different: private notebook jottings that record his attempts to grapple with some of the central ideas in Stoicism and to put them into practice in his own life.

The works of these three Roman Stoics have inspired readers ever since, speaking as they do to some of the day-to-day issues that face anyone trying to navigate their way through life. Their works, fundamentally, are about how to live – how to understand one's place in the world, how to cope when things don't go well, how to manage one's emotions, how to behave towards others, how to live a good life worthy of a rational human being. In the chapters that follow we'll explore some of these themes further. We'll begin by considering what the Stoics thought their philosophy could offer, namely a therapy for the mind. We'll explore what we can and cannot control, and how the way we think about things can generate sometimes harmful emotions. We'll then think about our relationship with the outside world and our place within it. And we'll conclude by focusing on our relationships with other people, which contribute so much to both the joys and the stresses of daily life. As we shall see, the popular image of the isolated and unfeeling stoic hardly does justice to the rich vein of thought that we find in our three Roman Stoics. Their works have been perennial classics, and for good reason. Their popularity remains undiminished today, with new generations finding helpful lessons in the works of these Stoics.

# 01

# The Philosopher as Doctor

**TOWARDS THE END** of the first century AD a former slave, originally from Asia Minor, whose real name we don't even know, set up a philosophy school in a new town on the western coast of Greece. He'd gone there not entirely through his own choice, having been banished from Rome – along with all the other philosophers – by the Emperor Domitian, who saw such intellectuals as a potential threat to his rule. The town was called Nicopolis, founded about a century earlier by Augustus, and the ex-slave was known by the name of Epictetus, which in Greek simply means 'acquired'. During the years of its operation, Epictetus's school attracted many students and eminent visitors, not least the Emperor Hadrian, who was far more favourably disposed towards philosophers than some of his predecessors had been. Epictetus himself wrote nothing, but one of his pupils – a young man named Arrian who would go on to become an important historian in his own right – took notes of the conversations in the school and later worked them up into the *Discourses of Epictetus*. In the *Discourses*, Epictetus is quite clear about what his role is as a philosopher. The philosopher, he says, is a doctor, and the philosopher's school is a hospital – a hospital for souls.

When Epictetus defined philosophy in this way he was following a well-established Greek philosophical tradition that extended back at least to Socrates. In Plato's early dialogues, Socrates had argued that the task of the philosopher is to take care of one's soul, just as a physician takes care of one's body. By 'soul' we ought not to assume anything immaterial, immortal or supernatural. Instead in this context we should understand it simply as mind, thoughts and beliefs. The task of the philosopher is to analyse and assess the things one thinks, examining their coherence and cogency. On this almost all philosophers, ancient or modern, would agree.

For Socrates, and later the Stoics, this concern with taking care of one's soul was all the more important because he and they held that the condition of our soul ultimately determines the quality of our lives. Socrates famously chastized his fellow Athenians for paying great attention to their bodies and their possessions but very little attention to their souls – to what they think or believe, to their values and characters. Yet Socrates insisted that the key to a good, happy life lies in attending to the latter, not the former.

In an important argument later taken up by the Stoics, Socrates sought to show that something like great wealth is, in a sense, worthless. To be more precise, he argued that material wealth is value-neutral, because it can be used for good or bad ends. The money in itself is neither good nor bad. Whether it is used for good or bad ends depends upon the character of the person who has it. A virtuous person can use money to do good things, while a not so virtuous individual might use it to generate great harm.

What does this tell us? It shows that the real value – the source of what is good or bad – resides in the *character* of the person who has the money, not in the money itself. It also tells us that paying excessive attention to our money and possessions while neglecting the state of our character is a grave mistake. It is the job of the philosopher to provoke us to see this, and then to support us as we try to cure our souls of whatever infirmities they may have.

One response to this line of thought would be to say that we should pay attention *only* to the state of our souls, and become indifferent to things like worldly success, money or reputation. Indeed, the Stoics called such things 'indifferents'. Only an excellent, virtuous character is genuinely good, they claimed, while only its opposite, a vicious character, is bad; everything else is a mere 'indifferent'. There were some philosophers who came after Socrates who thought just this. These were the Cynics, the most famous of whom was Diogenes of Sinope, who is said to have lived – for a while at least – in a barrel, like a stray dog. Diogenes pursued a virtuous, excellent character at the expense of everything else, advocating an austere, simple life in harmony with Nature. On seeing a child drinking water just using its hands, Diogenes is reported to have said, 'A child has beaten me in simplicity of living,' and then to have thrown away one of the few things he owned, his cup.

Zeno, the first of the Stoics, was for a time drawn to the Cynic way of life, but ultimately found it wanting. Socrates had said that money can be used for both good and bad ends, but if you've got no money at all you're unable to do any good with it. As Aristotle had remarked, some virtues seem to require a certain amount of wealth, such as generosity or charity. Not only that, but Diogenes's active dislike of possessions seemed to go beyond the claim that these things are mere 'indifferents'. If money really is an indifferent, then why care whether you are completely broke or stinking rich? Diogenes seemed to be saying that it was always better to be poor than wealthy. One can see how this praise of poverty would leave its mark on parts of the later Christian tradition.

But this was not Zeno's view. Diogenes had said we ought to live a life in harmony with Nature. Zeno's response was to say that it is completely natural for us to pursue things that help us to survive – food, shelter,

things that maintain our health, and possessions that contribute to our physical comfort.
We all do it, and there's no reason to feel bad
about it. We all pursue material prosperity
because it helps to secure our survival.

In everyday language we might say that
all these things that benefit us are 'good', but
Zeno, following Socrates, wanted to reserve
the word 'good' for an excellent, virtuous
character. So instead he said that they have
value. We value being healthy, well off and
respected, but nevertheless none of these
things are 'good' in the way that an excellent character is good. This led Zeno to call
these things 'preferred indifferents' in his
technical vocabulary. All other things being
equal, we'd all prefer to be rich rather than
poor, healthy rather than ill, and respected
rather than despised. Of course we would;
who wouldn't? But – and this is a key point
– because a virtuous character is the *only*
thing that is truly good, we ought never to
compromise our character in the pursuit of

such things. Nor ought we to think that any of these things can, on their own, make us happy. The person who pursues money, not simply to meet the needs for survival, but because they think that it will automatically give them a good, happy life, is gravely mistaken. The person who compromises their integrity in the pursuit of fame or money has made a graver mistake still, for they have damaged their character – the only truly good thing – for the sake of a mere 'indifferent'.

These are some of the things that Epictetus would have discussed at his school in Nicopolis. His pupils would have been predominantly the children of the Roman elite, about to embark on administrative careers in the Empire. One hopes that such lessons made them better than they would otherwise have been.

But just what does it mean to take care of one's soul? What is involved in having an excellent character? To use a very out-offashion word, it means to be virtuous. In particular it means to be wise, just, courageous and moderate – the four cardinal virtues according to the Stoics. This is what it means to have a good character and to be a good human being. While at first blush all this talk of 'virtue' might sound a bit moralistic, it is also possible to translate it into more descriptive terms. What is a good human being? Can we talk about good people in the same way we might talk about a good table or a good knife? A good table is one that meets the definition of providing a stable surface; a good knife is one that cuts well. If humans are by nature social animals, automatically born into families and communities, then a good human being will be one that behaves sociably. Someone who does not behave well towards others – who does not have the character traits of justice, courage and moderation – will in a sense fail to be a good human being, and if they fail completely we might even question whether they are really human at all. 'That person is a monster,' we might say about someone who has committed unspeakable crimes against others.

No one wants that. Indeed, the Stoics also followed Socrates in thinking that no one *chooses* to be vicious and unpleasant. Everyone pursues what they *think* is good, even if their idea of what's good or what will benefit them is hopelessly distorted. Again, that is where the philosopher comes in. The task of the philosopher, conceived as a doctor for the soul, is to get us to examine our existing beliefs about what we think is good and bad, what we think will benefit us, and what we think we need in order to enjoy a good, happy life.

According to the Stoics, a good, happy life is one that is in harmony with Nature. We'll come back to this idea a number of times in the chapters that follow. For now, we can say this involves both the thought that we should live harmoniously with the external natural world (Nature with a capital

'N') and in harmony with our own human nature. These days we are often encouraged to think that people are by nature selfish and competitive, always out for their own advantage. The Stoics have a quite different, more optimistic, view about human nature. Left to their own devices, the Stoics think that humans will naturally mature into rational, virtuous adults. We are by nature reasonable and decent social animals. Of course, many things can interrupt and interfere with that process of development, and when they do we find ourselves living a life out of sync with our deepest natural inclinations. When this happens, we become unhappy.

This is when we need the help of a philosopher-doctor, who can offer remedies that will enable us to get back on track. One of the things we hope these remedies will do is reconnect us with a sense of what we are as human beings and how we might live in the light of that knowledge. The first step towards this is to start to pay attention to the condition of our souls, just as Socrates exhorted, which is to say our beliefs, judgements and values. The first lesson, then, is that while there may well be external aspects of our lives that we might want to change, we need to pay close attention to how we think about things as well.

# 02

# What Do
# You Control?

**WHAT ASPECTS OF** your life do you really control? Do you control whether you get ill or not? Do you ever decide to be involved in an accident? Can you stop your loved ones dying? Do you get to choose whom you fall in love with and who falls in love with you? Can you guarantee your own worldly success? How much control do you really have over any of these things? You might be able to influence them in various ways, but can you ever guarantee that they will turn out in your favour? Questions such as these were a central preoccupation of the Stoics.

The *Handbook* of Epictetus opens with a fairly blunt account of what things he thinks are and are not 'up to us'. The things that we can control – the things in our power – include our judgements, impulses and desires. Pretty much everything else is, Epictetus suggests, ultimately out of our control, including our own bodies, our material possessions, our reputation and our worldly success. He goes on to say that much of human unhappiness is simply due to misclassification, the product of thinking that we have control over certain things when in fact we don't.

This division looks like it might involve a distinction between things that are either internal or external: we can control our minds but not the world around us. Or we might think of it as a distinction between the mental and the physical: we can control our thoughts but not material things such as our bodies or possessions. Neither of those ways of thinking about it are quite right, although both do capture something of what's going on. Epictetus does not say that we have control over everything internal to us or over all of our thoughts. Instead he claims that we have control only over a certain set of mental actions. To be more precise, he thinks that all we really have control over are our judgements, along with things that derive from our judgements. We don't have complete control over everything in our minds; we don't choose the sensations and memories that we have, and we cannot switch on and off our emotions (we'll come back to emotions in the next chapter). No, all we have complete control over are our judgements, which is to say what we think about the things that happen to us.

Now, our judgements are hugely important because, among other things, they determine how we act. As Epictetus put it, they control our desires and impulses. We might see something, make a judgement that it is something good, which creates a desire for it, which in turn prompts us to pursue it. Depending on what the thing is – a dream career, an expensive house – it might be a long and arduous pursuit, carried out at great cost to both ourselves and others. But the whole process begins with a simple act of judgement.

So, judgements are fundamental, and we neglect them at our peril, but we often make them so swiftly that we don't even notice that we are doing anything. We might judge so quickly that something is good, and do it so often, that we start to assume that the thing in question just *is* good in itself. But nothing external is inherently good; it's all just matter in motion. Only a virtuous character is genuinely good. The Roman Emperor Marcus Aurelius, who was an avid reader of Epictetus, often tried to remind himself of this by pausing to think about the physical nature of seemingly desirable things before passing judgement on them: a fine meal is merely the dead body of a pig or a fish. Equally, the expensive gadget or executive car is just a lump of metal and plastic. Whatever value these things might seem to have is value that we attribute to them with our judgements, and not anything inherent in the things themselves.

The good news, according to Epictetus, is that we have complete control over our judgements, and with some reflection and training we can soon overcome the tendency to judge things unthinkingly. If we can do that – if we can become masters of our own judgements – then we'll be in complete control of our lives. We'll decide what's important to us, what we desire and how we act. Our happiness will be completely within our own control. On the face of it Epictetus seems to be saying that we don't have control over very much at all, but in fact he is saying that we have control over everything that truly matters for our wellbeing.

What about all the other stuff that he says we don't control, all the stuff that preoccupies so much of our attention – our bodies, possessions, reputation and worldly success? We've already seen the Stoics argue that none of these things are inherently good. Epictetus's point here is slightly different. His point is that even if you think they *are* good, the fact is that you have no control over them. If you make your happiness dependent on one of these things, it will be extremely vulnerable to forces out of your control. Whether it be a romantic relationship, a specific career ambition, material possessions or a certain physical appearance, if your sense of wellbeing depends on one of these sorts of things, then you have effectively handed over your happiness to the whims of something or someone else. That's not a good position to be in. If you think you *do* have control over these things, when the plain fact is that you don't, then frustration and disappointment are almost guaranteed.

It is worth stressing here that Epictetus is not suggesting that we should give up on or turn away from the external world. Just because we cannot control something does not mean that we ought to ignore it. It's simply a matter of developing the right attitude towards it. Later on in his *Handbook*, Epictetus proposes thinking of your life as if you were an actor in a play. You haven't chosen your role, you don't get to decide what happens, and you have no control over how long it will last. Rather than fight against all these things which are out of your control, your task is to play the role you find yourself in as best as you can.

We should probably qualify this a bit. We all find ourselves assuming a number of roles. Some of these we can certainly change if we want to – no one is suggesting that it is compulsory to remain stuck in a miserable job or an unhappy relationship. But there are other things more closely tied to the human condition that we can't do much about. None of us have chosen our nationality, gender, age, skin colour or sexual orientation, yet all these things will have a significant impact on the shape of our lives.

It is also important to remember that, although we have control over our actions, we don't have control over their outcomes. Things don't always turn out the way we might have hoped or intended. Sometimes that's because we have not acted as well as we could, but equally often it's due to other factors out of our control. Antipater, a Stoic writing some time before Epictetus, drew an analogy with archery: even an expert archer will sometimes miss the target because the wind might blow his arrow off course. There's absolutely nothing the archer can do about this. The same goes for medicine: no matter how good doctors are, sometimes factors out of their control mean they are unable to save a patient. The Stoics think that all of life is like this. We can strive to act as best as we can, but we can never completely

control the outcome. If we tie our happiness
to achieving the outcome, we run the risk
of being frequently disappointed, but if we
make our goal simply doing the best we can,
then nothing can get in our way.

When it comes to events in the external
world, including the outcomes of our own
actions, all we can really do is go with the
flow. Accept what happens and work with
it rather than fight against it. Throughout
his *Meditations*, Marcus Aurelius repeatedly
reminds himself that Nature is in a continual process of change, nothing is stable, and
there is nothing that he can do about it. All
we can do is accept what happens that is not
within our control, while focusing our efforts
on those things that are.

Epictetus is particularly insistent on the
need to focus our attention on the things
that *are* within our control. Forget about the
things you can't control and direct all your
attention to your judgements, which will, in
turn, improve your character, which is the

one thing that will enable you to achieve
what Zeno called 'a smooth flow of life'. But
one must be vigilant, for if we stop paying
attention to our judgements even for a brief
moment we run the risk of falling back into
bad habits. Epictetus draws an analogy with
a mariner sailing a ship:

> It's much easier for a mariner to wreck his
> ship than it is for him to keep it sailing safely;
> all he has to do is head a little more upwind
> and disaster is instantaneous. In fact, he does
> not have to do anything: a momentary loss of
> attention will produce the same result.

If we let our attention slip we can quickly
lose whatever progress we may have made.
So, we need to integrate periods of reflection into our daily lives. Marcus Aurelius
describes practices of morning reflection
during which he prepares himself for the
coming day, contemplating the sorts of
challenges he is likely to face so that he
will be better placed to handle them. Sim-

ilarly, Seneca outlines a process of evening reflection during which he goes over his day, thinking about what he did well, where his attention may have slipped, and how he might do better tomorrow. Epictetus goes even further: like the mariner sailing the ship, it is essential that we remain focused every single moment of the day, prepared for whatever might happen next. We must keep our key philosophical principles always ready to hand, so that we don't fall back into making mistaken judgements. This is philosophy as a daily practice and a way of life.

# 03

# The Problem
# with Emotions

**ARRIAN REPORTS AN** encounter between Epictetus and a man who was visiting his school in Nicopolis that illustrates further this concern with control. The man asks Epictetus what he can do about his brother, who has become angry with him. What can the man do about his brother's anger? Epictetus's typically to-the-point reply is 'Nothing; you can do nothing about it.' We cannot control other people's emotions, because they fall into the category of things not up to us. The only person that can do anything about the brother's anger is the brother himself. But Epictetus doesn't just leave it there; he shifts attention to what the man *can* control, namely his own reaction to his brother's anger. The man is upset by his brother's anger and Epictetus suggests that *this* is the real problem here, but also that it is something the man can himself fix. The man has made a judgement about his brother's anger, and that judgement has generated an emotion of the man's own that has upset him. The immediate problem, then, is not with the brother, but with the man who has come to complain.

This little story illustrates the ways in which emotions – both others' and our own – can shape and colour our interactions with the people around us. In modern English the word 'stoic' has come to mean unfeeling and without emotion, and this is usually seen as a negative trait. Emotions these days are more often than not taken to be good things: love, compassion, sympathy, empathy are surely all things of which the world could do with more. But this story highlights other emotions – anger, resentment, impatience – that are not so attractive. When the ancient Stoics recommended that people ought to avoid emotions, it was these negative emotions that they primarily had in mind.

The Stoic account of emotions is on one level very easy to understand, but there are a number of important qualifications we must add in order to grasp it fully. The central claim is simply this: our emotions are the product of judgements we make. Consequently we are in complete control of our emotions and responsible for them. The man is upset about his brother's anger because of the attitude he takes to it. If he viewed it differently, he would not have got upset. The Stoic claim – and this is an important point – is not that we should deny or repress our emotions; it is rather that we should try to avoid having them in the first place. A second important point is that the Stoics don't think that someone can just click their fingers and make an emotion go away. You can't just say, 'I'm going to think about this differently,' and see one's anger or grief magically disappear.

Chrysippus likened having an emotion to running too fast. Once you have a certain amount of momentum, you cannot simply stop. Your motion is out of control, and being in the grip of an emotion is very much like this. So, you can't simply turn off an unwanted emotion at will, but what you can do is try to avoid letting the next one pick up momentum to the point that it becomes out of control.

This seems clear in the case of anger. When someone is angry, really angry, the emotion takes over and you can no longer reason with them. One person who knew about this all too well was Lucius Annaeus Seneca, originally a native of Spain. His career as an adviser in the inner circles of the Roman imperial court involved frequent confrontations with people in the grip of destructive emotions which were compounded by the fact that some of these people – such as the emperors Caligula, Claudius and Nero – literally had the power of life and death over countless individuals, not least Seneca himself. Caligula was so jealous of Seneca's varied talents that he ordered his death at one point, only to be talked down by one of his intimates on the grounds of Seneca's poor health.

In his essay *On Anger* Seneca describes emotions such as anger and jealousy as a temporary madness. Picking up Chrysippus's image of running so fast that one cannot stop, Seneca likens being angry to having been thrown off the top of a building and hurtling towards the ground, completely out of control. Once anger takes over, it compromises the whole mind. It's being in this condition of being completely out of control that the Stoics warn against. Being a bit annoyed from time to time is simply part of life and does little real harm. Being so angry that one can no longer resist the urge to hit someone is quite another matter, and this is what the Stoics want to avoid.

Seneca insists that we don't need anger to respond to acts committed against us or our loved ones. It's always better to act calmly from a sense of loyalty, duty or justice than to rage for revenge. If on occasion anger might seem to spur us on to, say, fight against some great wrongdoing, Seneca says it would be much better to do the same thing under the guidance of the virtues of courage and justice.

Anger, like all emotions, is the product of a judgement made in the mind. That means it is something we can control, or at least it is something that we can try to avoid in the future. But once a judgement has been made, anger soon becomes something tangible and physical. Seneca describes anger as a disease of the body characterized by swelling. Whatever the emotion might be, we can probably think of numerous physical symptoms: heart racing, temperature rising, palpitations, sweating, and so on. Once these are in play there's nothing we can do to make them go away except wait.

Contrary to the popular image, the Stoics do not suggest that people can or should become unfeeling blocks of stone. All humans will experience what Seneca calls 'first movements'. These are when we are moved by some experience, and we might feel nervous, shocked, excited or scared, or we might even cry. All these are quite natural reactions; they are physiological responses of the body, but not emotions in the Stoic sense of the word. Someone who is upset and momentarily contemplates vengeance, but does not act on it, is not angry according to Seneca, because he remains in control. To be momentarily scared of something, but then remain firm, is not the emotion of fear either. For these 'first movements' to become emotions proper would require the mind judging that something terrible has happened and then acting on it. As Seneca puts it, 'fear involves flight, anger involves assault.'

There are thus three stages to the process, Seneca suggests: first, an involuntary first movement, which is a natural physiological reaction out of our control; second, a judgement in response to the experience, which is within our control; third, an emotion that, once created, is out of our control. Once the emotion is there, there is nothing we can do but wait for it to subside.

Why do we make the judgements that generate these harmful emotions? If you think that you've been injured in some way by another person, it might seem perfectly natural to become angry with them. Seneca says that anger is usually the product of a sense of injury. So the thing that must be challenged is the impression that some injury has happened, which already contains within it a judgement. Epictetus puts it like this:

Remember, it is not enough to be hit or insulted to be harmed, you must believe that you are being harmed. If someone succeeds in provoking you, realize that your mind is complicit in the provocation.

This is why, he continues, it is important not to react impulsively to events. It is essential to pause, take a moment and reflect on what has just happened before making a judgement about it. If someone says something critical about you, stop to consider whether what they say is true or false. If it is true, then they have pointed out a fault that you can now address. As such, they have benefited you. If what they say is false, then they are in error and the only one being harmed is them. Either way, you suffer no harm from their critical remarks. But the one way in which their remark *could* cause you a real and serious harm is if *you* were to let it provoke you into a state of anger.

Seneca focused his attention on destructive negative emotions such as anger. But anger isn't the only emotion out there. Surely there are other emotions that are not so destructive, emotions that are in fact mainly positive and that we would not want to live without. One obvious candidate would be love, both the love a parent has for their child and romantic love between two adults. Are the Stoics suggesting that we do away with these?

According to the Stoics, a parent's love for their child is not an irrational emotion best avoided; instead, it is a more or less universal natural instinct. We are by nature inclined to care for ourselves, pursue those things we need to live and avoid those things that might harm us, all for the sake of self-preservation. That instinct for self-preservation soon extends to those close to us – first to our close family members, but ideally to all other people. As for romantic love, perhaps we might say that a healthy relationship is one based on natural desires for companionship and procreation, while unhealthy ones are based on negative emotions of possessiveness and jealousy. The Stoics certainly do not envisage turning people into unfeeling blocks of stone.

So, we'll still have the usual reactions to events – we'll jump, flinch, get momentarily frightened or embarrassed, cry – and we'll still have strong caring relationships with those close to us. What we won't do, however, is develop the negative emotions of anger, resentment, bitterness, jealousy, obsession, perpetual fear or excessive attachment. These are the things that can ruin a life and that the Stoics think are best avoided.

# 04

# Dealing with Adversity

**SOMETIMES BAD THINGS** happen. This is part of life. Even if we are prepared to take on board Epictetus's lesson that many of these things are just out of our control, that won't automatically lessen the blow. I might fully accept that I have complete control only over my judgements, and ultimately no control over whether I become physically ill, but that in itself might not stop me thinking that my physical illness is something really bad, a genuine adversity.

For the Roman Stoics life is full of adversity, and one of the central tasks of philosophy is to help people navigate through the ups and downs of life. No one knew this better than Seneca, whose own life was far from the ideal of calm tranquillity to which he aspired. During the tumultuous first century AD Seneca had to contend with the death of his son, exile to Corsica for the best part of a decade, rescue from exile (but only on condition that he take up the role of tutor to the young Nero), a career as adviser to Nero from which he wasn't easily able to leave, the death of a close friend and, to top it all off, his own forced suicide. Suspected of being part of a plot against the Emperor, Nero demanded the death of his old tutor. Seneca's wife insisted on sharing his fate, and they both cut their arms. Neither died quickly. His wife, Paulina, survived, while Seneca was given hemlock and eventually a steaming bath to finish him off. This was certainly not a quiet 'philosophical life'.

Seneca's own account of how one ought to approach adversity was actually written quite early on in his life, well before many of the adversities just mentioned. It can be found in his essay *On Providence*, which he wrote when he was about forty years old. Nero had only just been born and Seneca was yet to be sent away to Corsica. But around this time his father died and he came into conflict with the Emperor Caligula, avoiding execution only owing to his poor health, as we have seen. Illness, threat of death, bereavement – and things hadn't even started to get bad. Seneca is sometimes presented as a privileged hypocrite, an immensely wealthy member of the elite who had the cheek to extol the benefits of a simple life. He was certainly fortunate in many ways, with opportunities that the vast majority of his contemporaries could barely dream of, but he also had his fair share of adversity and he spent a lot of time thinking about how to deal with it.

His essay focuses on the question of why it is that people suffer so much misfortune.

Seneca responds to this from a number of different directions. First, he insists that nothing bad ever really happens, given that all external events are neither good nor bad in themselves. Someone who keeps this idea in their mind and doesn't rush to hasty judgement will simply accept what happens for what it is, without judging that something terrible has occurred.

However, Seneca goes further. Not only does he think that we ought not to see apparent misfortunes as genuinely bad; he also thinks that we ought to welcome them as things that can benefit us. The good person, he says, treats all adversity as a training exercise. Seneca draws an analogy with a wrestler who benefits from taking on tough opponents, and who would lose his skill if he only ever faced weaker challengers. The wrestler only gets to prove his skill when facing a real adversary, and a tough match also acts as training so that he can develop his talents. Adversity in life works in a similar way: it lets us display our virtues and it trains them so that we can improve. If we can see this, then we'll happily welcome adversity when it comes.

Seneca draws a further analogy with soldiers, making references to a wide range of famous historical examples. Just as a general will only send his finest soldiers into the most difficult battles, so too will God send the toughest challenges only to the most worthy individuals. To experience adversity, then, is a mark of having a virtuous character.

Conversely, excessive good fortune is in fact really bad for us. When are we ever tested if we never experience any difficulties? How will we ever develop the virtues of patience, courage or resilience if everything always goes well? There is no worse luck, Seneca says, than unending luxury and wealth, which will serve only to make us lazy, complacent, ungrateful and greedy for more. This is real misfortune! By contrast, whatever adversity life throws at us will always be an opportunity to learn something about ourselves and to improve our characters.

All this looks at first glance as if it depends on belief in a providential deity. People who believe in such a thing can hopefully take away something useful from what Seneca says. But what about those who don't? Is all this merely empty talk if one does not believe in a tough but kindly God? We might also wonder whether Seneca himself believed in such a God. He wrote his essay in the late 30s AD, well before Christianity had really got going. Although a series of letters supposed to be between Seneca and St Paul circulated during the Middle Ages, they are no longer thought to be genuine, and it's unlikely that Seneca had any knowledge of the newly emerging religion. So Seneca's God is the Stoics' God, which they identified with the animating rational principle in Nature. Their God is not a person but rather a physical principle that accounts for the order and organization of the natural world (we'll come back to this in the next chapter). When Seneca refers to the 'will of God', then, he is referring to this organizing principle, which the Stoics identified with fate and, in the words of Cicero, Stoic fate is the fate of physics, not superstition.

Given all this, how literally ought we to take Seneca's description of a tough father sending us tests? Might all this just be for rhetorical effect? Without getting too lost in questions about Seneca's own theological beliefs, there is, I think, a way to approach what Seneca says about adversity that can stand regardless of one's own religious views. Whether one believes in a benevolent deity, pantheistic order or atomic chaos, it remains entirely up to us whether we choose to see an event as a disaster or an opportunity. Is getting sacked from one's job a calamity or a chance to do something new? Although such a thing happening is inevitably a challenge – no one is pretending you can just ignore the very real practical consequences – there is a

choice to be made between seeing it *as if* it is
a terrible blow or *as if* it is a positive challenge. That's simply up to us. We can also
see here a difference in emphasis between
Seneca and Epictetus. Whereas Seneca proposes that we think of seemingly bad things
as in fact good (or at least beneficial), Epictetus counsels that we pay minimal attention
to such events, instead keeping our focus
squarely on our own judgements.

Seneca knew all too well about adversity
from his own life. His attempt to draw out
some positives from his experiences was no
doubt one of a number of things he did to
help him cope in difficult circumstances. As
he wrote to his mother, Helvia, while in exile
on Corsica, 'everlasting misfortune does have
one blessing, that it ends up by toughening
those whom it constantly afflicts'. The lan-
guage he uses in *On Providence* can sometimes make it sound as if he relished the
fight, ready to welcome the next onslaught
for the benefits he could take from it. But

in one of his letters to his friend Lucilius he strikes a quite different tone:

> I do not agree with those who recommend a stormy life and plunge straight into the breakers, waging a spirited struggle against worldly obstacles every day of their lives. The wise man will put up with these things, not go out of his way to meet them; he will prefer a state of peace to a state of war.

No one in their right mind goes out looking for adversity, even if it can teach us some useful lessons along the way. But developing the skills to cope with it when it does come – as it surely will – can only be to our advantage. It falls hardest, Seneca says in his letter to his mother, on those who don't expect it, but is much easier to cope with if one is prepared for it. This idea is developed in another letter of consolation, this time to Marcia, a friend who had been battling with grief. She had lost one of her sons some three years earlier, but her suffering hadn't really subsided. The natural period of mourning was over and now her grief had become a debilitating habit of mind. It was time for an intervention.

The most interesting part of Seneca's response to this situation is his account of what is sometimes called the premeditation of future evils. This was something advocated by earlier Stoics, such as Chrysippus. The idea is that one should reflect on potentially bad things that *could* happen, so that one is better ready to handle them if they ever did happen. Part of Marcia's problem, Seneca suggests, is that she never adequately reflected on the possibility of her son's death. Yet we all know that from the moment of birth everyone is destined to die. This isn't something that merely *could* happen, it is something that necessarily *will* happen.

Grief hits people hard, Seneca says, because they don't anticipate it. We see and hear of death and misfortune affecting others all the time, especially in our era of

rolling news, yet rarely do we stop to contemplate how *we* might respond in similar
circumstances. Seneca tells Marcia – and
us – a whole series of things that we might
prefer not to hear: we are all vulnerable;
our loved ones will inevitably die, and could
do so at any time; whatever prosperity and
security we have could be taken away at any
moment by forces beyond our control; even
when we think things are really tough, it is
always possible for them to get still worse.
How prepared would we be to cope if luck
turned against us? Would we react as calmly
and indifferently as we often do when we see
such things reported in the news happening
to strangers far away? In those cases we tend
simply to acknowledge such suffering as part
and parcel of life, something regrettable but
inevitable. It's easy to be 'philosophical' when
it's not happening to us or to our loved ones,
but what about when it's our turn?

It is simply illogical, Seneca says, to think,
about some misfortune, 'I didn't think it

would happen to me,' especially when one knows that it could happen and one has seen it happen to many others. Why not you? In the case of grief, it is even more illogical, given the inevitability of death for all living things. It has to happen at some time, so why not now? It's irrational to expect one's luck to hold out for ever. Seneca thinks that reflecting on adversities that *might* happen along with those that *must* at some point happen can help to lessen the blow if or when they do strike us. It can reduce the shock and help to make us better prepared to cope. In effect, what Seneca is advising is that we prepare for every eventuality, including those that we'd rather did not happen and prefer not to think about. We shouldn't just assume that everything will work out as we hope or expect, for it's unlikely to do so. This is an important, if uncomfortable, lesson.

**05**

# Our Place in Nature

IN COMPARISON WITH Seneca's, the life of Marcus Aurelius was relatively calm. Although his father died when he was very young, he was adopted into the imperial family as a teenager, and eventually became Emperor in AD 161, a month before his fortieth birthday, remaining so until his death in 180. His reign is widely considered to be one of the better periods of Roman imperial history, although for Marcus much of it was spent at war on the northern fringes of the Empire shoring up its borders. It was

towards the end of his life, while on cam-
paign in Germania, not far from modern-
day Vienna, that Marcus kept a notebook in
which he wrote to himself in an effort to process the experiences of each day and to prepare himself for the next.

His *Meditations* have attracted countless readers since they were first printed in
the late sixteenth century, from Frederick
the Great to Bill Clinton. But they have not
appealed only to people who, like Marcus,
have found themselves struggling with the
pressures of leadership at the highest level.
Anyone can pick up his book and find inspi-
ration, such as the young man who wrote to
me once to comment, 'I'm 23, life is hard and
confusing, don't know my purpose, Marcus's
*Meditations* helped me a lot.' He is but one
of many who have found the *Meditations* a
helpful, if not life-saving, source of guidance.
One of the reasons for this, I think, is that
readers find they can identify with Marcus,
who comes across as all too human, grap-

pling with the pressures of daily life, workplace responsibilities and social gatherings. Marcus might have been Roman Emperor, and subsequently might have gained a reputation as a wise Stoic philosopher, but the reality we encounter in the *Meditations* is simply a late-middle-aged man doing his best to cope with the demands of life.

One of the central themes that threads itself through the *Meditations* is fate. This brings us back to Epictetus's concern with control. Marcus had read the *Discourses* as a young man, and their influence can be seen throughout his own writings. But whereas Epictetus turned his attention inwards, to focus on what we can control, Marcus looked outwards to contemplate the vastness of what we cannot. Again and again Marcus reflects on his own life as but one tiny moment in the vastness of time, and his own body as a mere speck in the vastness of the universe:

What a tiny part of the boundless abyss of
time has been allotted to each of us – and this
is soon vanished in eternity; what a tiny part
of the universal substance and the universal
soul; how tiny in the whole earth the mere
clod on which you creep.

Elsewhere Marcus imagines looking down
on the earth from a great height – as astro-
nauts have since done – and seeing how tiny
each country is and how minuscule great cities are. As for the people living in those cities,
with lives full of cares and concerns, they are
practically nothing when viewed from such
a cosmic perspective. From such a vantage
point it can feel as if the universe doesn't care
about us, and why should it.

Strictly speaking, this is not the Stoic
view. The Stoics didn't think that Nature
is an indifferent mass of matter in motion.
As we saw in the last chapter, Seneca presents Nature as being under the control of
a paternalistic deity. The official Stoic view

is that there is a rational principle within Nature, responsible for its order and animation. They call this 'God' (Zeus), but it is not a person, and nothing supernatural – it simply *is* Nature. Nature isn't blind and chaotic; it is ordered and beautiful, with its own rhythms and patterns. It is not composed of dead matter; it is a single living organism, of which we are all parts.

If this sounds potentially at odds with what modern science tells us about Nature, we might try to draw a parallel with what is known as the Gaia hypothesis, developed by James Lovelock. The idea is that life on earth is best understood as a single living system, including not just obviously organic matter but also inorganic things like rocks and the atmosphere. It's a mistake to try to understand organisms like plants and animals in isolation. This single, unified biosphere regulates itself, acting, so to speak, for its own benefit. Lovelock defines it as:

a complex entity involving the Earth's bio-sphere, atmosphere, oceans, and soil; the totality constituting a feedback or cybernetic system which seeks an optimal physical and chemical environment for life on this planet.

Like all scientific theories, this is aimed at offering the best explanation of the available evidence. It proposes some form of organiz-ing principle within Nature that acts for the benefit of life. It can be explained in techni-cal scientific terms – a cybernetic system – or presented more poetically as 'Gaia'. The Stoic view of Nature shares much in common with this late-twentieth-century scientific theory, which is also sometimes described in purely physical terms but sometimes in the lan-guage of Greek theology. For the Stoics, 'God' and 'Nature' are just two different names for the same single living organism that encom-passes all things.

Stoic Nature, conceived as an intelligent organism, is governed according to fate.

By 'fate' the Stoics simply mean a chain of causes. The natural world is governed by cause and effect, and that is what physics tries to describe and understand. For Stoics such as Marcus, accepting the reality of fate – of causal determinism – is essential. It's not just that some things are out of our control; it's that they couldn't be any other way. You might acknowledge that you couldn't control the outcome of some key event, all the while wishing that it had turned out other than it did. But the Stoics will insist that not only was it not in your control, it couldn't have turned out any other way, given the various causes at play at that moment.

This might start to sound a bit fatalistic: how can we tiny specks of matter do anything in the face of the overpowering forces that shape the world? That would be a false impression, though, for the Stoics certainly didn't advocate that kind of passivity. Our actions can and do make a difference. They can themselves be causes at play that contribute to the outcome of events. As one ancient source put it, fate works *through* us. We are ourselves *contributors* to fate and parts of the larger natural world governed by it. But that doesn't change the fact that when an event happens, given the various causes at play, the outcome could not have been otherwise. It is fruitless, then, to wish that things had turned out other that they did. Marcus puts it like this:

> Nature gives all and takes all back. To her the man educated into humility says: 'Give what you will; take back what you will.' And he says this in no spirit of defiance, but simply as her loyal subject.

For the Stoics, thinking about fate is a central element in the remedy for adversity, because part of coming to terms with unpleasant events is accepting that they *had* to happen. Once we grasp that something was inevitable, we shall see that bemoaning it is pointless, will only generate further distress and simply displays a failure to grasp the way the world works.

This attitude that we find in Marcus Aurelius contains a shift in emphasis from what we saw previously in Seneca. While Seneca stressed the providential order within Nature, Marcus focuses more on the inevitability of events. In a number of passages in his *Meditations*, he appears to express agnosticism on whether Nature is a rational, providential system or merely a random accumulation of atoms banging together in an infinite void. Marcus was no physicist, and his duties as emperor hardly left him time to investigate the matter in detail himself. In any case, his final view was that for practical purposes it doesn't matter a great deal. Whether Nature is ruled by a providential deity, a cybernetic feedback system or blind fate, or is simply the chance product of atomic interactions, the response from us should always be the same: accept what happens and act in response as best we can.

Having said that, elsewhere in the *Meditations* – in passages written on different days, in different moods, and in the light of different events in his own life – Marcus appears much clearer in his own view:

> Universal Nature's impulse was to create an orderly world. It follows, then, that everything now happening must follow a logical sequence; if it were not so, the prime purpose towards which the impulses of the World-Reason are directed would be an irrational one. Remembrance of this will help you to face many things more calmly.

Whether Nature is providentially ordered for our benefit or not, as Seneca claimed, Marcus thinks that grasping that there is at least some kind of order and reason for what happens can help us to cope with whatever comes our way. There's always some kind of reason for what happens, even if it is simply the inevitable consequence of the pre-existing states of affairs combined with the laws of physics.

There are other features of the physical world that Marcus also thinks we ought to pay close attention to in our daily lives. The following passage is worth quoting at length:

> Make a habit of regularly observing the universal process of change; be assiduous in your attention to it, and school yourself thoroughly in this branch of study; there is nothing more elevating to the mind. For when man realizes that at any moment he may have to leave everything behind him and depart from the company of his fellows, he casts off the body and thenceforward dedicates himself wholly to the service of justice in his personal actions and compliance with Nature in all else. No thought is wasted on what others may say or think of him or practise against him; two things alone suffice him, justice in his daily dealings and contentment with all fate's apportionings.

The lesson here is that we are but parts of Nature, subject to its greater forces and inevitably swept along by its movements, and we shall never be able to enjoy a harmonious life until we fully comprehend this.

# 06

# Life and Death

**NONE OF US** know when or how we shall die, but we do know that one day all of this that we currently experience will come to an end. How many of us live our lives fully conscious of this knowledge? Most of us are familiar with stories of people who have had close encounters with death or have been diagnosed with a life-threatening illness, only to come out the other side with a renewed and revitalized appreciation of life and the time that they have left. For those of us who haven't been through such an experience it is easy to forget our own mortality and the all too limited amount of time that we have left.

As we saw earlier, Seneca was no doubt conscious that his own life could come to an end at any moment, either through ill health or a bad-tempered emperor. This led him to reflect on the value of time and how best to use it. Perhaps surprisingly, he insisted that all of us have more than enough time, no matter how long or short our lives turn out to be; the problem is that we waste most of it. The idea that time is the most valuable thing we have may sound like just another obvious platitude, but once again we might reflect on how many of us actually live with this knowledge truly in mind.

In his essay *On the Shortness of Life*, Seneca says that, for many of us, by the time we are really ready to start living, our lives are almost over. It's not that our lives are too short; the problem is that we waste so much time. We procrastinate, pursue things of little or no value, or wander aimlessly through life with no clear focus. Some people strive to achieve success so that they can be wealthy enough to buy luxury goods that will end up discarded in a rubbish bin long before their lives are done. In so doing they waste the greater part of their lives. Others strive for nothing, just going through the motions of daily routines without any sense that the most valuable commodity they have – time – is slipping away. Some people have a clear idea of what they want to do but, paralysed by fear of failure, put off and delay things and conjure up excuses for why now is not the time to act. All these different types, Seneca says, fail to live.

It is only in rare moments that most people really feel alive. The bulk of life is reduced to merely passing time. So what's the remedy? How does Seneca think we can take control of our lives and live them to the full?

First of all we should stop worrying about what others think. Don't try to impress others; don't pursue their favour in order to secure some advantage. Too many people care about what others think of them, but pay little attention to their own thoughts. They sacrifice their time to others but rarely set aside time for themselves. Yet it's absurd, Seneca suggests, that someone might be so protective of their money and possessions and yet so freely give away their far more valuable time.

We also need to hold in our minds the brute fact that we shall die. Our time is not unlimited. A good part of whatever time we shall have is gone already. Not only that, we have no idea how much is left to come. Today could, in fact, be your last day. Perhaps tomorrow will be your last. You might have weeks, months, a couple of years – the truth is that none of us know. It is all too easy to assume that we'll all make it to eighty or ninety years old, but perhaps not all of us will. The assumption may be false and, whether it is or not, it encourages us to put off things into a future that may never come. Seneca mocks the person who postpones all their plans and dreams until retirement. Do you really know you'll make it to then? If you do, are you sure you'll be in good enough health to do whatever it is that you've been postponing for so long? But even if all goes well, why postpone life until the bulk of it is already over?

There's also the question of what's worth pursuing. For a good many people, the goal is success in some form or other, whether that be wealth and fame, respect and honours, or promotion and high office. Yet Seneca notes that, more often than not, people who attain such things are far from satisfied, for with success comes a whole host of demands and pressures. Having gained everything they ever wanted, there's one thing they now lack: time, time for themselves, for peace and quiet, leisure and retirement.

But it is not just the demands that come with success. It is all too easy to live in a perpetual state of distraction, never fully attending to what it is that we should be doing, what we really want to be doing, or even the sheer experience of being alive. Constant noise, interruption, news, media, social media – all these things can demand our attention to the point that it becomes difficult to focus enough to complete anything. As Seneca puts it, 'living is the least important activity of the preoccupied man'. They are effectively taken up with doing nothing. Once this habit develops they fall into a continual state of restlessness, unable to relax or to concentrate on anything. Such people become fully conscious of the value of life only when it is almost over.

If we don't address these issues, Seneca argues, it doesn't matter how much longer our lives continue. Even if we lived for a thousand years, we'd fritter most of the time away. The task, then, is not to strive to make our lives last as long as possible; instead, we ought simply to make sure that we enjoy and make full use of each day as it comes, not forgetting that it could perhaps be our last.

Learning to live well is, paradoxically, a

task that can take a lifetime. The wisest people of the past, Seneca adds, gave up the pursuit of pleasure, money and success in order to focus their attention on this one task. Although they might not have agreed on an answer, Seneca insists that preserving one's time and devoting it to oneself is essential:

> Everyone hustles his life along, and is troubled by a longing for the future and weariness of the present. But the man who spends all his time on his own needs, who organizes every day as though it were his last, neither longs for nor fears the next day.

This idea of living one's life as if each day is the last might sound a bit morbid; it might also seem to preclude planning for the future. It's worth stressing that Seneca isn't suggesting that we try to think that this *really is* our last day. Instead, he is reminding us to contemplate the fact that it *could be*. We just don't know when all this will end, and that's the problem. If we knew that we had just one year left, we could at least plan and organize our remaining time accordingly, making sure no moment is wasted. But without that sense of urgency, it becomes all too easy to waste it all.

With this renewed sense of the value of time and a determined effort to prioritize our own leisure, what does Seneca think we ought to do? He quickly dismisses the playing of games and sports, as well as the popular holiday activity of what he calls 'cooking one's body in the sun'. Indeed, he attacks many of the things that are often referred to today as 'leisure activities'. Instead, he recommends philosophy as the finest and most worthy activity, by which he means thinking, learning, reading history and literature, reflecting on the past and the present. This is the opposite of rushing around in the pursuit of worldly success, which, he says, is 'won at the cost of life'.

Seneca's essay is a polemic against what he saw as the shallowness of the culture of the relatively wealthy in first-century Rome.

It is striking – in some ways frighteningly so – how relevant all this remains today. We like to think that humanity has moved on, and hopefully improved, over the last two thousand years, but Seneca shows us that many of the issues that people grapple with today are no different from those that preoccupied the inhabitants of imperial Rome.

Around fifty years after Seneca was writing, Epictetus reflected on life and death with his students in Nicopolis. In the records of those discussions Epictetus repeatedly describes life as a gift, something that has been given to us, but equally something that can be taken away. It does not belong to us but instead to the giver, Nature. Addressing this higher power, he says:

> Now you want me to leave the fair, so I go, feeling nothing but gratitude for having been allowed to share with you in the celebration.

Life is an event, like a fair or a party, and like all such events it must come to an end. It is up to us whether we thank the host for a good time or bemoan the fact that it cannot go on for longer.

Your own life, then, is a gift, and one day you will have to give it back. The same goes for the lives of your loved ones:

> Under no circumstances ever say 'I have lost something', only 'I returned it'. Did a child of yours die? No, it was returned. Your wife died? No, she was returned.

Everything that we have and that we love is merely on loan. Nothing can be kept for ever, not least because we will not be here for ever. It is tempting to present this as a tragic, bittersweet truth about human existence, but Epictetus himself is far more blunt about it:

> You are a fool to want your children, wife, or friends to be immortal; it calls for powers beyond you, and gifts not yours to either own or give.

In a very matter-of-fact way Epictetus says that death, whether our own or someone else's, is nothing terrible, for if it were, Socrates would have thought it so. The fact that figures renowned for wisdom have faced death with equanimity ought to give us pause for thought, he suggests. The belief that death is something terrible is merely the product of our judgement about it. We can choose to think about it differently. Indeed, Epictetus insists that we *ought* to think about it differently, because the judgement that it is something terrible rests on a mistake. The brute fact of being alive is an indifferent, and, in any case, one of the things not within our control.

In all this Epictetus's goal is to reduce our anxiety about death and to soothe our grief at the loss of loved ones. But just like Seneca he also wants us to appreciate the life that we have. Your life does not belong to you, it could be taken away at any moment, so enjoy it while it lasts. Towards the end of his *Handbook*, Epictetus likens life to the Olympic games: the contest is upon us, you cannot defer any longer, and everything depends on what you do right now, on this single day.

# 07

# How We Live Together

**MUCH OF WHAT** we have seen so far has been self-focused – self-centred and selfish, a critic might say. Epictetus's division between what we can and cannot control seems to counsel turning our backs on the outside world in order to focus attention on our judgements. In a memorable image Marcus Aurelius described retreating into his 'inner citadel' in order to escape the external world. Is this sort of retreat from the outside world, ignoring everyone else, in order to focus simply on our own wellbeing, really what the Stoics suggest?

Not at all. We are not individual, isolated entities; we are parts of Nature. The Stoics would also agree with Aristotle when he said that human beings are by nature social and political animals. We are born into communities: immediately, into our family, but also into our local community, our country, and ultimately into the community of all humankind. Moreover, the Stoic turn inwards, as we have already seen, is primarily focused on cultivating good, virtuous character traits and avoiding harmful, antisocial emotions, such as anger. The whole point of it is that afterwards we turn back outwards to play our parts as more effective members of the various communities of which we are necessarily a part.

Indeed, it is Epictetus who stresses most the fact that each of us inhabits a number of different social roles. Some of these roles come to us from Nature, he suggests. The role of being a parent isn't something that has been socially constructed, for we can see the way animals look after their offspring, just as we do. Then there are other, slightly different, roles connected to social positions or jobs that we may have. Someone who takes on the role of a doctor or a magistrate, for instance, commits themselves to a range of duties and responsibilities that come with the role, and we tend to judge quite harshly someone who abuses or neglects these sorts of important positions. So, if we want to live a good life, we need to be good human beings. That means embracing our nature as rational and social beings. But it also means living up to the various roles that we find ourselves in and accepting the responsibilities that come with them.

Epictetus gives a good example of this. A man of some importance came to visit his school in Nicopolis. He was a magistrate, and so presumably had some sense of the sorts of duties and responsibilities that come with certain roles. The man was also a father. On being asked about the wellbeing of his family, the man responded by saying that his daughter had been so gravely ill that he couldn't bear to stay with her and see her in such a condition. So he had run away. Epictetus chides him for two things: selfishly obsessing about his own feelings while neglecting those of others, not least his daughter's, and neglecting his role as a father. Epictetus also challenges the inconsistency of his behaviour, for he certainly wouldn't want *everyone* to abandon his daughter when she was ill, leaving her all alone, and he wouldn't want everyone to abandon him if he were ill. He claims to have fled due to his love for his daughter when, as her father, his love for her should have made him stay. He failed to fulfil his role.

Beyond specific roles, such as being a parent, we might also think more broadly about being a member of a much wider community of people, and most broadly of all as simply being a member of the human race. Does this involve any duties or responsibilities?

The Stoics think it does. We have a duty of care to all other human beings, and they suggest that as we develop our rationality we shall come to see ourselves as members of a single, global community of all humankind. A slightly less well-known Stoic of the imperial period called Hierocles (about whose life we know almost nothing) outlined in his treatise on Stoic ethics the idea that we are each at the centre of a series of expanding circles of concern, starting with ourselves, then containing our immediate family, then our local community and eventually ending with the largest circle that embraces all humankind. The modern idea of cosmopolitanism, then, has its origins with the Stoics.

It is worth noting, though, that this does not mean that you should neglect your place within your local community. In a famous passage, Seneca put it like this:

> Let us grasp the idea that there are two
> commonwealths – the one, a vast and truly

common state, which embraces alike gods and
men, in which we look neither to this corner
of earth nor to that, but measure the bounds
of our citizenship by the path of the sun; the
other, the one to which we have been assigned
by the accident of birth.

The key thing to note here is that we are
members of *both* communities, with responsibilities to our local community but also
with a duty of care to all humankind that
transcends local customs and laws. On occasions where the two might come into conflict,
the latter must come first, but that doesn't
make the former go away.

Indeed, there was a long tradition of Stoic
involvement in politics in Rome. In the first
century AD Seneca was far from being the
only Stoic to come into conflict with various
emperors, and, like him, a good number lost
their lives at the hands of Nero. One such
figure was Helvidius Priscus, a tribune, prae-
tor and member of the Senate. A student of

philosophy in his youth, Helvidius was, like
Seneca, exiled on more than one occasion,
first for his political associations and later
for his own criticisms of the Flavian regime.
He is remembered in particular for standing
up to the Emperor Vespasian, and Epictetus
recounts their confrontation. When Helvidius saw Vespasian abusing the authority of
the Senate, he refused to back down. Warned
to stay away, Helvidius insisted on standing
up to the Emperor to defend his rights – and
indeed those of all members of the Senate.
He was executed for his troubles.

Rather than run away from his role as
a senator or his duty to his community,
Helvidius was prepared to die for a point of
political principle. Later, Marcus Aurelius
would name Helvidius alongside a number
of other Stoic martyrs as one of the people
who taught him 'the conception of a community based on equality and freedom of speech
for all, and a monarchy concerned primarily
to uphold the liberty of the subject'.

As well as thinking about traditional politics and how to play his role as Emperor well, Marcus also engaged with the idea of a larger community embracing all humankind. We are all parts of a single community, parts of a single organism, like branches of a tree, he suggested. In order to remain parts of that wider community we must remain on good terms with all the other members:

> A branch cut off from its neighbouring branch is necessarily cut away from the whole tree. In the same way a human being severed from just one other human has dropped from the whole community. Now the branch is cut off by someone else, but a man separates himself from his neighbour by his own hatred or rejection, not realizing that he has thereby severed himself from the wider society of fellow citizens.

No one can be happy when isolated and cut off from other people; it is simply against our nature as social animals.

What we have seen thus far would suggest that the Stoics were committed to equality between all people. This was a topic touched on by another Roman Stoic whom we have not encountered yet. His name was Musonius Rufus, a native of Italy, who lectured on philosophy in Rome in the first century AD. Epictetus attended his lectures and mentions him a number of times in the *Discourses*. So too did the Stoic opponents murdered by Nero.

Like Seneca, Musonius suffered at the hands of multiple emperors, exiled by both Nero and Vespasian on different occasions. For a while he was banished to the barren Greek island of Gyara, waterless until Musonius himself discovered a spring. He was not without company, though, for before too long admirers would travel there to see him.

We have reports of a number of his lectures, which, as in the case of Epictetus, were written down by an admiring student. In one of those lectures Musonius is asked if women should be allowed to study philosophy. He responds by saying that women have just the same powers of reasoning as men, and indeed the same natural inclination towards virtue. He suggests that women – just as men – can benefit from studying the sorts of topics we have already considered in the previous chapters.

While that might not seem like a particularly radical idea today – indeed, it might seem more than a little patronizing – it's worth remembering that things like universal education and voting rights for women are not much more than a hundred years old, yet Musonius argued for at least some form of gender equality some two thousand years ago. For the Stoics, then, people are people, all equal in their shared rationality and instinct for virtue.

This focus on sociability and equality challenges the idea that Stoics were indifferent to other people. But even so, that needn't mean that we ought to be surrounded by other people all the time. In fact, Epictetus warned against the company of other people, especially if someone is trying to make a change in their life. It's very difficult to try to break free from old habits or destructive patterns of behaviour if we are surrounded by other people still living that way. As Epictetus put it, if you brush up against someone covered in soot, you're going to get covered in soot yourself.

Epictetus was addressing his students in Nicopolis who, like many university students today, were away from home and about to head back for the vacation. Should they catch up with their old schoolfriends if they are trying to break free from some aspects of their previous way of life? The risk is that they will fall back into past habits, returning to their old patterns of behaviour in order to fit in. Epictetus advises them to be extremely cautious, recommending that they avoid the company of others as much as possible until the new habits they want to develop have become properly embedded.

This needn't lead to social isolation, though. There are some people that it's good to spend time with: people with good habits, people following the same path as you, people who understand and value what you are trying to do. The recovering alcoholic can find encouragement at his support group but only temptation among his old drinking companions. Epictetus suggests that we should think of all of life like this and that we ought to consider very carefully whom we spend time with, what influence they might have on us, how we might unwittingly end up aping what they think and do.

So, if you are trying to develop some new, positive habits, it may be best to avoid the company of those whose lives embody everything you are trying to escape. Instead, try to spend time with those whose values you share or admire. This is one of the reasons why philosophers in antiquity tended to group together into schools. It also probably stands behind the monastic traditions of various world religions. It is why aspiring Stoics gathered together in antiquity, in places such as Epictetus's school, and it's why today people who want to draw on Stoicism in their daily lives are often keen to make contact with others trying to do the same, either in person or online. Despite Epictetus's warning against spending time with the wrong kind of company, he also gives good reasons why learning from the Stoics can benefit from being a social affair.

Our final lesson is that we are by nature parts of a whole series of communities, both local and global. We are simply mistaken if we think of ourselves as isolated individuals who can ignore wider society. In Rome, committed Stoics were prepared to face up to tyrants rather than compromise their principles. In so doing they embodied the virtues of courage and justice. Far from counselling political passivity, Stoicism encourages us to live up to the very highest standards of political action.

# Epilogue

**MANY OF THE** ideas that we have considered are neatly summed up in a passage by Seneca in the letter of consolation he sent to his mother, she bewailing the loss of her son, he stranded on Corsica, not knowing what the Emperor Claudius's next move against him might be.

> It was Nature's intention that there should be no need of great equipment for a good life: every individual can make himself happy. External goods are of trivial importance and

without much influence in either direction: prosperity does not elevate the sage and adversity does not depress him. For he has always made the effort to rely as much as possible on himself and to derive all delight from within himself.

These ideas have resonated down the ages ever since. Seneca was widely read during the Middle Ages, the Renaissance and well into the eighteenth-century Enlightenment. Epictetus's short *Handbook* was adapted for use as a guide for monks in the early medieval period. Marcus Aurelius's *Meditations* became a bestseller in Victorian England and has remained one of the most popular philosophy books ever since. Many of the fundamental Stoic ideas that we have discussed were important influences on the development of forms of cognitive behavioural therapy in the mid-twentieth century, such as Rational Emotive Behaviour Therapy.

Since 2012 over 20,000 people have taken part in a global online experiment to see if living like a Stoic for a week might improve their sense of wellbeing. The results suggest that it does. Those who have followed a month-long experiment saw even greater benefits. Against all the stereotypes, the character trait that increases most for people following Stoic guidance is zest, a feeling of energy and enthusiasm for life.

We can, I hope, all benefit from thinking about the issues that the Stoics addressed. But the real benefit comes, they would insist, only if we incorporate these ideas into our daily lives. This is where the really hard work begins.

# Further Reading

**THE WORKS OF** the three Roman Stoics are widely available in modern translations. Among these the following volumes can be found in Penguin Classics:

Epictetus, *Discourses and Selected Writings*, trans. Robert Dobbin, 2008

Marcus Aurelius, *Meditations*, trans. Martin Hammond, 2006

Seneca, *Dialogues and Letters*, trans. C. D. N. Costa, 1997

Seneca, *Letters from a Stoic*, trans. Robin Camp-
    bell, 1969

All three can also be found in the Penguin
Great Ideas series:

Epictetus, *Of Human Freedom*, trans. Robert
    Dobbin, 2010
Marcus Aurelius, *Meditations*, trans. Maxwell
    Staniforth, 2004
Seneca, *On the Shortness of Life*, trans. C. D. N.
    Costa, 2004

Readers who would like to delve further
into Seneca can find all of his works freshly
translated, with notes, in the series *The
Complete Works of Lucius Annaeus Seneca*,
published by the University of Chicago Press,
2010–17.

A number of books have been written
highlighting ways in which people might
make use of Stoic ideas today; these include,
in order of publication:

William Irvine, *A Guide to the Good Life*, Oxford University Press, 2009

Donald Robertson, *Stoicism and the Art of Happiness*, Hodder & Stoughton, 2013

Ryan Holiday and Stephen Hanselman, *The Daily Stoic*, Profile, 2016

Massimo Pigliucci, *How To Be a Stoic*, Rider, 2017

Readers interested in learning more about the Roman Stoics might look at:

Pierre Hadot, *The Inner Citadel: The Meditations of Marcus Aurelius*, Harvard University Press, 1998

A. A. Long, *Epictetus: A Stoic and Socratic Guide to Life*, Oxford University Press, 2002

Emily Wilson, *Seneca: A Life*, Allen Lane, 2015

Readers curious to learn more about the philosophy of Stoicism, especially in the hands of the earlier Athenian Stoics, might begin with:

Brad Inwood, *Stoicism: A Very Short Introduction*, Oxford University Press, 2018

John Sellars, *Stoicism*, 2006, repr. Routledge, 2014

There are numerous websites and other online resources devoted to Stoicism. I shall mention just one, www.modernstoicism.com, run by the team who also run 'Stoic Week', an annual experiment that invites people to live like a Stoic for a week in order to see what impact it might have on their sense of wellbeing, and 'Stoicon', an annual gathering of people interested in drawing on Stoicism in their daily lives.

# References

**CHAPTER 1** Epictetus refers to the philosopher's school as a hospital at *Discourses* 3.23.30. Socrates draws the analogy between the philosopher and the doctor in Plato's *Alcibiades* 127e–130c, and he exhorts people to take care of their souls in Plato's *Apology* 29d–30b. He argues that external goods have no inherent value in Plato's *Euthydemus* 278e–281e. On Diogenes of Sinope living in a barrel and embracing the simplicity of living, see Diogenes Laertius, *Lives of the Philosophers* 6.23 and 6.37. Aristotle discusses generosity in *Nicomachean Ethics* 4.1. Zeno's views on external goods are reported in Diogenes Laertius 7.102–7.

**CHAPTER 2** Epictetus's distinction between things that are and are not in our power is in *Handbook* 1. Marcus Aurelius gives a physical description of objects in *Meditations* 6.13. On thinking of yourself as an actor in a play, see Epictetus's *Handbook* 17. Antipater's analogy with archery can be found in Cicero, *On Ends* 3.22. Marcus comments on universal change in *Meditations* 2.17. Zeno's phrase 'a smooth flow of life' is reported in Diogenes Laertius 7.88. Epictetus's 'It's much easier for a mariner . . .' is from *Discourses* 4.3.5. For morning and evening reflections, see Marcus's *Meditations* 2.1 and Seneca's *On Anger* 3.36.1–3. Epictetus insists on continual attention in *Discourses* 4.12.

**CHAPTER 3** Epictetus replies to the man with the angry brother in *Discourses* 1.15.

Chrysippus's description of runaway emotions is reported in Galen, *On the Doctrines of Hippocrates and Plato* 4.2.15–18. Caligula's hatred of Seneca is reported in Dio Cassius 59.19. Seneca refers to emotions as temporary madness in *On Anger* 1.1.2. For the analogy with hurtling to the ground see *On Anger* 1.7.4. On first movements, see *On Anger* 2.2.4–2.3.5. He says 'fear involves flight . . .' in *On Anger* 2.3.5. Epictetus's passage 'Remember, it is not enough . . .' is from *Handbook* 20.

**CHAPTER 4** Seneca's death at the order of Nero is recounted in Tacitus's *Annals* 15.60–64. Seneca presents adversity as a training exercise in *On Providence* 2.2; the analogy with wrestling is at 2.3 and the one with soldiers is at 4.8. Cicero refers to the fate of physics in his *On Divination* 1.126. Seneca writes 'everlasting misfortune . . .' in his *Consolation to Helvia* 2.3. The passage from Seneca's letter, 'I do not agree with . . .' comes from *Letters to Lucilius* 28. His comment on being prepared for adversity is in *Consolation to Helvia* 5.3. He reflects on preparing for future adversity in *Consolation to Marcia* 9.1–2.

**CHAPTER 5** Marcus writes 'What a tiny part . . .' in *Meditations* 12.32. For an example of Marcus Aurelius's view from above, see *Meditations* 9.30. James Lovelock outlines his Gaia hypothesis in *Gaia: A New Look at Life on Earth* (Oxford University Press, 1979; repr. 2000); the quotation is from p. 10. The image of fate working through us comes from Alexander of Aphrodisias, *On Fate* 181,14. Marcus writes 'Nature gives all . . .' in *Meditations* 10.14; he contrasts providence with atoms in 9.39 among other places. 'Universal Nature's impulse . . .' comes from *Meditations* 7.75; 'Make a habit . . .' is from 10.11.

**CHAPTER 6** The quotation 'living is the least important activity . . .' is from Seneca's *On* *the Shortness of Life* 7.3; 'everyone hustles . . .' is at 7.8–9; 'won at the cost of life' is at 20.1. The first quotation from Epictetus, 'Now you want me to leave the fair . . .', is from *Discourses* 3.5.10; 'Under no circumstances . . .' is from *Handbook* 11; 'You are a fool . . .' is from *Handbook* 14.

**CHAPTER 7** Marcus describes retreating into his 'inner citadel' in *Meditations* 8.48. Aristotle describes humans as political animals in his *Politics* 1.2. The account of the man with the sick daughter is in *Discourses* 1.11. Hierocles's circles of concern can be found in a fragment preserved in Stobaeus 4,671,7–673,11. The quotation from Seneca, 'Let us grasp . . .', comes from *On Leisure* 4.1. Epictetus remembers Helvidius Priscus in *Discourses* 1.2.19–21. Marcus Aurelius writes 'the conception of a community . . .' in *Meditations* 1.14 and 'A branch cut off . . .' in 11.8. The exile of Musonius Rufus is reported in Philostratus's *Life of Apollonius* 7.16.

Musonius advocates the study of philosophy for women in his *Diatribes* 3 and 4. Epictetus discusses the danger of associating with people who have bad habits in *Discourses* 3.16 and 4.2.

**EPILOGUE** The passage from Seneca comes from *Consolation to Helvia* 5.1. Readers curious about the later influence of Stoicism might look at John Sellars, ed., *The Routledge Handbook of the Stoic Tradition* (Routledge, 2016).

# Acknowledgements

**FIRST AND FOREMOST,** I should like to thank Casiana Ionita for suggesting that I write this book, as well as for her astute comments along the way and her stylistic fine-tuning of my initial drafts.

I should also like to acknowledge my collaborators in the Modern Stoicism team: Christopher Gill, Donald Robertson, Tim LeBon, and others past and present. It is unlikely that this book would have been written without the work that we have done together over the past few years and continue to do.

Last, but by no means least, I dedicate this book to Dawn, *sine qua non*.